COMPOSER SHOWCASE
HAL LEONARD
STUDENT PIANO LIBRARY

Miniatures in Style

SIX ORIGINAL PIANO SOLOS
In Baroque, Classical, Romantic, Impressionist, and Contemporary Styles

BY MONA REJINO

ON THE COVER:

A Lady Seated at a Virginal (1670–72), Johannes Vermeer

Manuela González Velázquez, Playing the Piano (1820), Zacarías González Velázquez

Chopin Performing in the Guest-Hall of Anton Radziville in Berlin in 1829 (1887), Henryk Siemiradzki

At the Piano (1908), Childe Hassam

ISBN 978-1-4950-2832-8

HAL•LEONARD®
CORPORATION
7777 W. BLUEMOUND RD. P.O. BOX 13819 MILWAUKEE, WI 53213

In Australia Contact:
Hal Leonard Australia Pty. Ltd.
4 Lentara Court
Cheltenham, Victoria, 3192 Australia
Email: ausadmin@halleonard.com.au

Visit Hal Leonard Online at
www.halleonard.com

Bourrée in G Major

Mona Rejino

Allegro risoluto (♩ = 88)

poco a poco cresc.

f

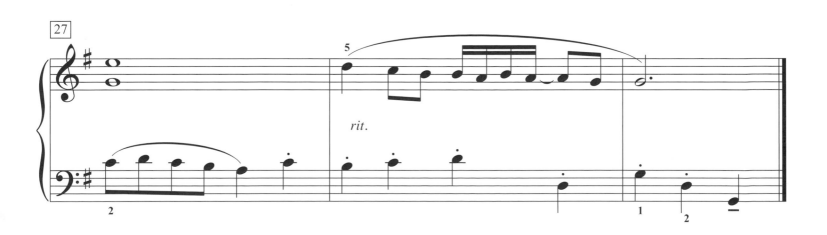

mf

rit.

3

Menuet in G Major

Mona Rejino

Allegro grazioso (♩. = 52)

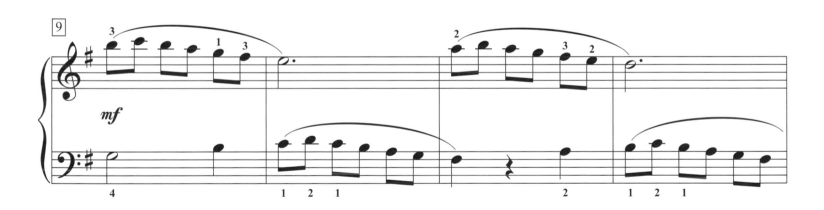

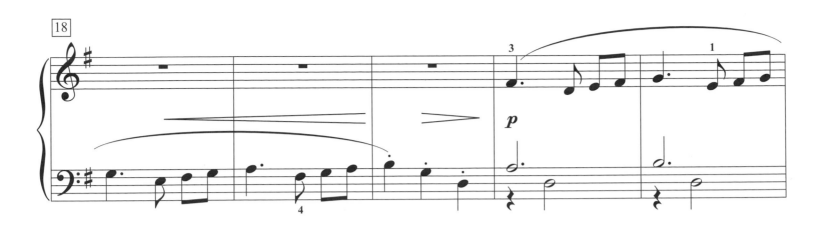

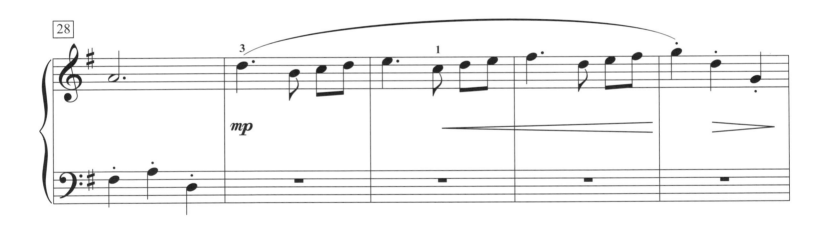

Classical Sonatina in C Major

I

Mona Rejino

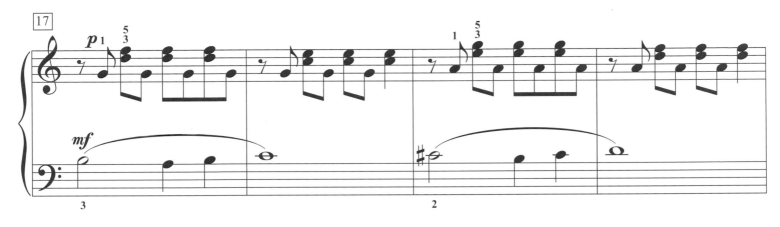

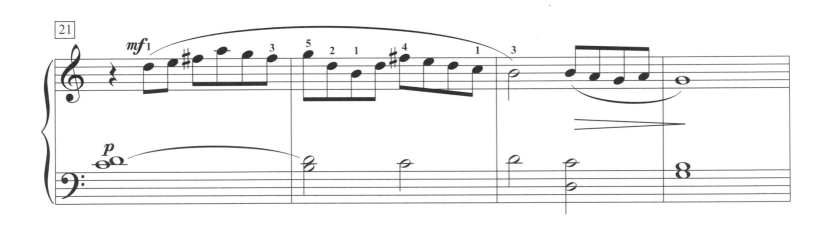

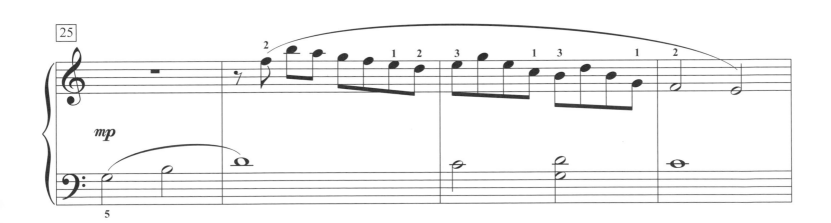

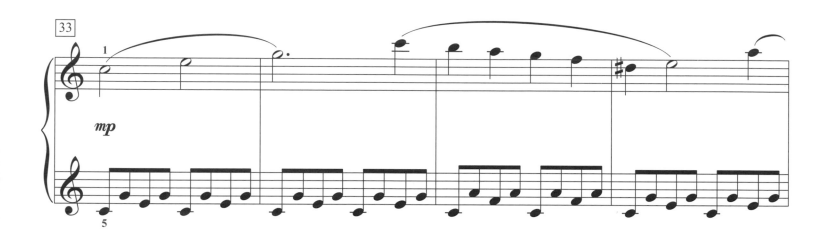

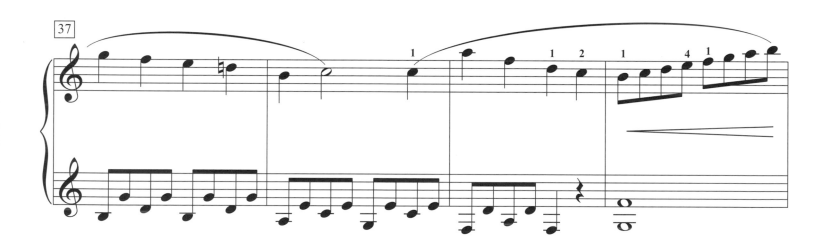

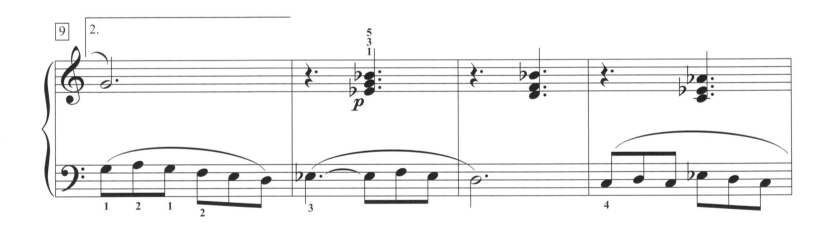

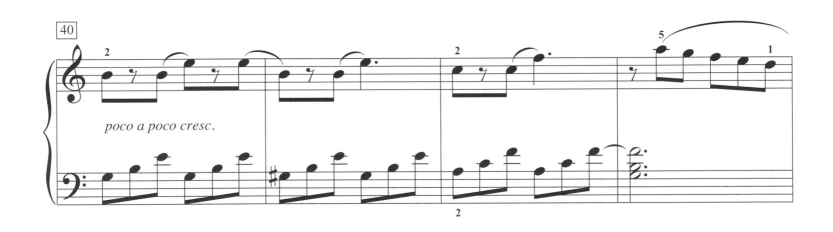

13

Shimmering Sea

Mona Rejino

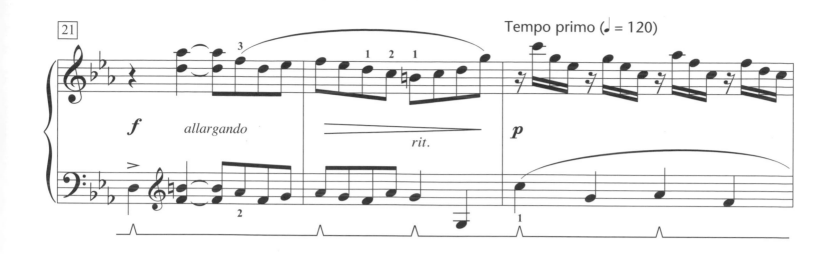

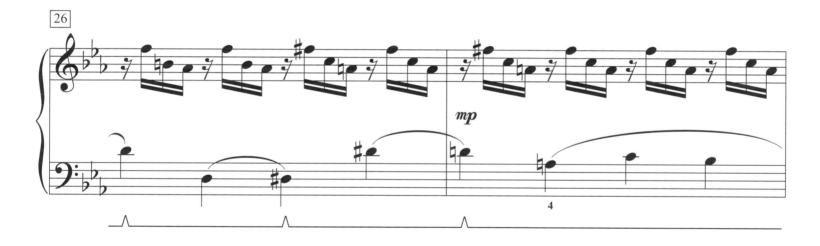

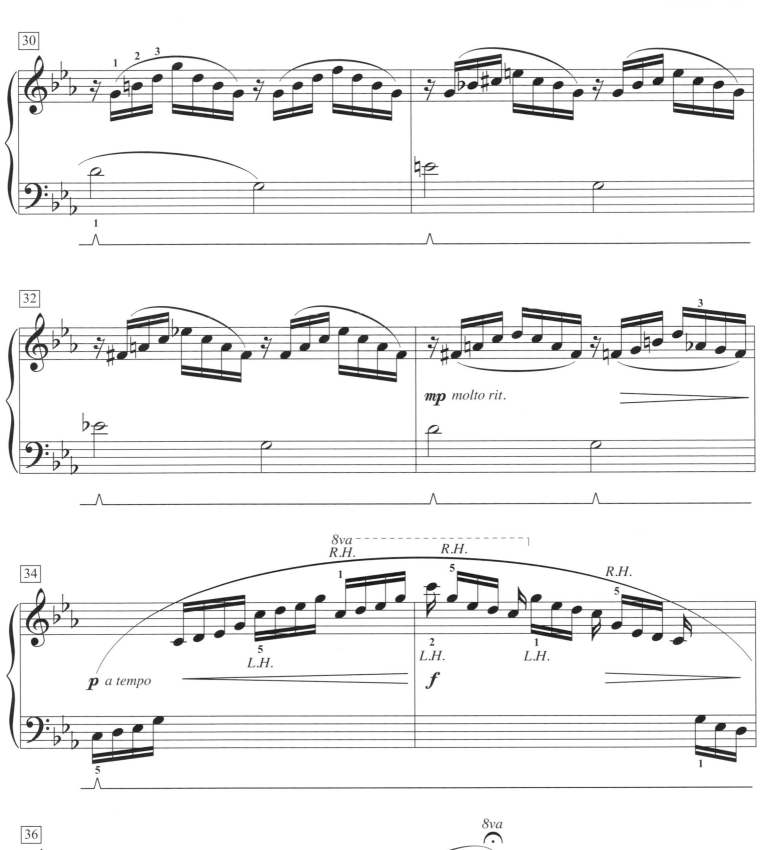

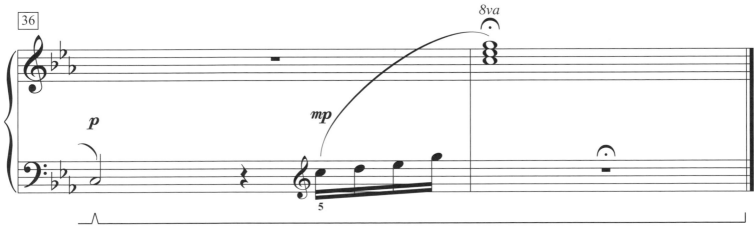

Romance

Mona Rejino

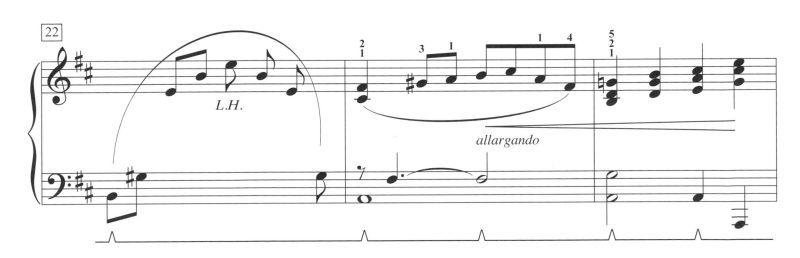

Aurora
(New Dawn)

Mona Rejino

Moderato (♩ = 100)

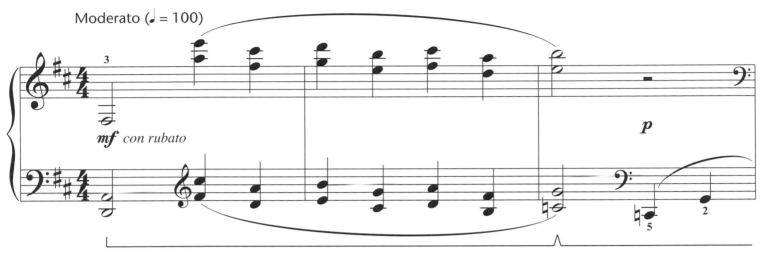

COMPOSER SHOWCASE
HAL LEONARD STUDENT PIANO LIBRARY

This series showcases great original piano music from our **Hal Leonard Student Piano Library** family of composers. Carefully graded for easy selection.

BILL BOYD

JAZZ BITS (AND PIECES)
Early Intermediate Level
00290312 11 Solos.............................$7.99

JAZZ DELIGHTS
Intermediate Level
00240435 11 Solos............................$8.99

JAZZ FEST
Intermediate Level
00240436 10 Solos............................$8.99

JAZZ PRELIMS
Early Elementary Level
00290032 12 Solos............................$7.99

JAZZ SKETCHES
Intermediate Level
00220001 8 Solos..............................$8.99

JAZZ STARTERS
Elementary Level
00290425 10 Solos............................$7.99

JAZZ STARTERS II
Late Elementary Level
00290434 11 Solos............................$7.99

JAZZ STARTERS III
Late Elementary Level
00290465 12 Solos............................$8.99

THINK JAZZ!
Early Intermediate Level
00290417 Method Book......................$12.99

TONY CARAMIA

JAZZ MOODS
Intermediate Level
00296728 8 Solos..............................$6.95

SUITE DREAMS
Intermediate Level
00296775 4 Solos..............................$6.99

SONDRA CLARK

THREE ODD METERS
Intermediate Level
00296472 3 Duets.............................$6.95

MATTHEW EDWARDS

CONCERTO FOR YOUNG PIANISTS
FOR 2 PIANOS, FOUR HANDS
Intermediate Level Book/CD
00296356 3 Movements $19.99

CONCERTO NO. 2 IN G MAJOR
FOR 2 PIANOS, 4 HANDS
Intermediate Level Book/CD
00296670 3 Movements......................$17.99

PHILLIP KEVEREN

MOUSE ON A MIRROR
Late Elementary Level
00296361 5 Solos..............................$8.99

MUSICAL MOODS
Elementary/Late Elementary Level
00296714 7 Solos..............................$6.99

SHIFTY-EYED BLUES
Late Elementary Level
00296374 5 Solos..............................$7.99

HAL•LEONARD®
www.halleonard.com

CAROL KLOSE

THE BEST OF CAROL KLOSE
Early Intermediate to Late Intermediate Level
00146151 15 Solos............................$12.99

CORAL REEF SUITE
Late Elementary Level
00296354 7 Solos..............................$7.50

DESERT SUITE
Intermediate Level
00296667 6 Solos..............................$7.99

FANCIFUL WALTZES
Early Intermediate Level
00296473 5 Solos..............................$7.95

GARDEN TREASURES
Late Intermediate Level
00296787 5 Solos..............................$8.50

ROMANTIC EXPRESSIONS
Intermediate/Late Intermediate Level
00296923 5 Solos..............................$8.99

WATERCOLOR MINIATURES
Early Intermediate Level
00296848 7 Solos..............................$7.99

JENNIFER LINN

AMERICAN IMPRESSIONS
Intermediate Level
00296471 6 Solos..............................$8.99

ANIMALS HAVE FEELINGS TOO
Early Elementary/Elementary Level
00147789 8 Solos..............................$8.99

CHRISTMAS IMPRESSIONS
Intermediate Level
00296706 8 Solos..............................$8.99

JUST PINK
Elementary Level
00296722 9 Solos..............................$8.99

LES PETITES IMAGES
Late Elementary Level
00296664 7 Solos..............................$8.99

LES PETITES IMPRESSIONS
Intermediate Level
00296355 6 Solos..............................$7.99

REFLECTIONS
Late Intermediate Level
00296843 5 Solos..............................$8.99

TALES OF MYSTERY
Intermediate Level
00296769 6 Solos..............................$8.99

LYNDA LYBECK-ROBINSON

ALASKA SKETCHES
Early Intermediate Level
00119637 8 Solos..............................$7.99

AN AWESOME ADVENTURE
Late Elementary Level
00137563..$7.99

FOR THE BIRDS
Early Intermediate/Intermediate Level
00237078..$8.99

WHISPERING WOODS
Late Elementary Level
00275905 9 Solos..............................$8.99

MONA REJINO

CIRCUS SUITE
Late Elementary Level
00296665 5 Solos..............................$6.99

COLOR WHEEL
Early Intermediate Level
00201951 6 Solos..............................$8.99

JUST FOR KIDS
Elementary Level
00296840 8 Solos..............................$7.99

MERRY CHRISTMAS MEDLEYS
Intermediate Level
00296799 5 Solos..............................$8.99

MINIATURES IN STYLE
Intermediate Level
00148088 6 Solos..............................$8.99

PORTRAITS IN STYLE
Early Intermediate Level
00296507 6 Solos..............................$8.99

EUGÉNIE ROCHEROLLE

CELEBRATION SUITE
Intermediate Level
00152724 3 Duets (1 Piano, 4 Hands)...............$8.99

ENCANTOS ESPAÑOLES
(SPANISH DELIGHTS)
Intermediate Level
00125451 6 Solos..............................$8.99

JAMBALAYA
Intermediate Level
00296654 Ensemble (2 Pianos, 8 Hands).........$12.99

JAMBALAYA
Intermediate Level
00296725 Piano Duo (2 Pianos) $7.95

LITTLE BLUES CONCERTO
FOR 2 PIANOS, 4 HANDS
Early Intermediate Level
00142801 Piano Duo (2 Pianos, 4 Hands).......$12.99

TOUR FOR TWO
Late Elementary Level
00296832 6 Duets.............................$7.99

TREASURES
Late Elementary/Early Intermediate Level
00296924 7 Solos..............................$8.99

JEREMY SISKIND

BIG APPLE JAZZ
Intermediate Level
00278209 8 Solos..............................$8.99

MYTHS AND MONSTERS
Late Elementary/Early Intermediate Level
00148148 9 Solos..............................$7.99

CHRISTOS TSITSAROS

DANCES FROM AROUND THE WORLD
Early Intermediate Level
00296688 7 Solos..............................$8.99

LYRIC BALLADS
Intermediate/Late Intermediate Level
00102404 6 Solos..............................$8.99

POETIC MOMENTS
Intermediate Level
00296403 8 Solos..............................$8.99

SEA DIARY
Early Intermediate Level
00253486 9 Solos..............................$8.99

SONATINA HUMORESQUE
Late Intermediate Level
00296772 3 Movements $6.99

SONGS WITHOUT WORDS
Intermediate Level
00296506 9 Solos..............................$9.99

THREE PRELUDES
Early Advanced Level
00130747 ....$8.99

THROUGHOUT THE YEAR
Late Elementary Level
00296723 12 Duets............................$6.95

ADDITIONAL COLLECTIONS

AT THE LAKE
by Elvina Pearce
Elementary/Late Elementary Level
00131642 10 Solos and Duets...........................$7.99

COUNTY RAGTIME FESTIVAL
by Fred Kern
Intermediate Level
00296882 7 Rags..............................$7.99

LITTLE JAZZERS
by Jennifer Watts
Elementary/Late Elementary Level
00154573 Solos....................................8.99

PLAY THE BLUES!
by Luann Carman (Method Book)
Early Intermediate Level
00296357 10 Solos............................$9.99

Prices, contents, and availability subject
to change without notice.